NOTES FROM THE WEST POLE

This book is dedicated to Diane Wells,
my beloved, who shared this journey.

SPECIAL THANKS

Eleanor Cooney
Hal and Sidra Stone
Judy Tarbell
Michael Lott
Anthony Wells
Tansy Chapman
Bob Santos
Ron Nadeau
Peter Temple
Joan Moore

Copyright © 2018 by Peter Wells
All rights reserved.

Published by Harmonyus
PO Box 185
Mendocino, CA 95460

Edited from the Notebooks of Peter Wells
by Michael Francis Lott

Cover Art, Photography & Typesetting
by Anthony Wells

ISBN 978-1-7324204-0-3

First Printing November, 2018
Printed in the United States of America

Notes From The West Pole is also available
as an audiobook, read by author Peter Wells:

harmonyus.com/audiobooks

FOREWORD

BY MICHAEL FRANCIS LOTT

Notes from the West Pole is about a change in our consciousness. It sheds light on how a human being divides the self, while also providing answers as to how to heal the division and make the person whole. This healing occurs through a shift in self-perspective. It requires letting go of the ideas of judgement and division that we acquire from the social system, and replacing those ideas with the reality of the indivisible soul.

I came across this material at a very significant point in my life, as several years ago I had left the mainstream world of academia and had decided to abandon everything to take a journey in search of myself. Through following a stream of synchronistic events, I happened to meet Peter Wells while plodding through the misty rolling hills of Northern California. I soon became fully immersed in his material. In his journals were inscriptions about healing the divided self, taking an inward journey to uncover one's soul, and of healing a divided world. As I became more immersed in this material, I saw so much of my own journey in these writings. I realized that he was striking upon deeply universal themes of self development, and that a guidebook was being revealed to me. As I digested this material, I could feel parts of my psyche being rewired, as it was attuning me to an expanded awareness of myself.

I know, from the inside out, the significant role that this material plays in shifting us out of a limited view of ourselves, and into an acceptance of the Wholeness. This material operates on many levels, as it speaks to both the individual and the collective process of integrating a new realization of who we are.

It is my deep honor to present you with this powerful work, as we make this passage together into new horizons of human understanding.

> *The West Pole was discovered by a restless young man from London, England, who went west, and west again, to explore the western extremity of our consciousness.*

TABLE OF CONTENTS

8	Borders of our Perception
19	That November Mood
26	The Oneness
29	The Oracle
33	Original Innocence
36	The Labyrinth
43	Make the Divided Thing Whole
50	Boy on the Beach
52	Soul Consciousness
57	Early Sorrows
63	The Inward Journey
67	Early Morning Grey and Still
74	The Intelligence
78	The Inner Person
81	The Game is Up
86	It's Not Out There, It's in Here
90	Evolutionary Event
91	Renaissance
97	Forbidden Journey
99	The Cage
102	Out From the Darkness of a Conquered Life
104	The Three Steps
108	A New Story

Notes From The West Pole

BORDERS OF OUR PERCEPTION

Here we are then, you and I
having left the cave
and tamed the animals,
having sown the seed
and grown
from village tribe, to city state,
to a world of warring nations.
Now we wait at the borders of our perception,
waiting for the vision
to go beyond the nation,
to be one human family on this earth.

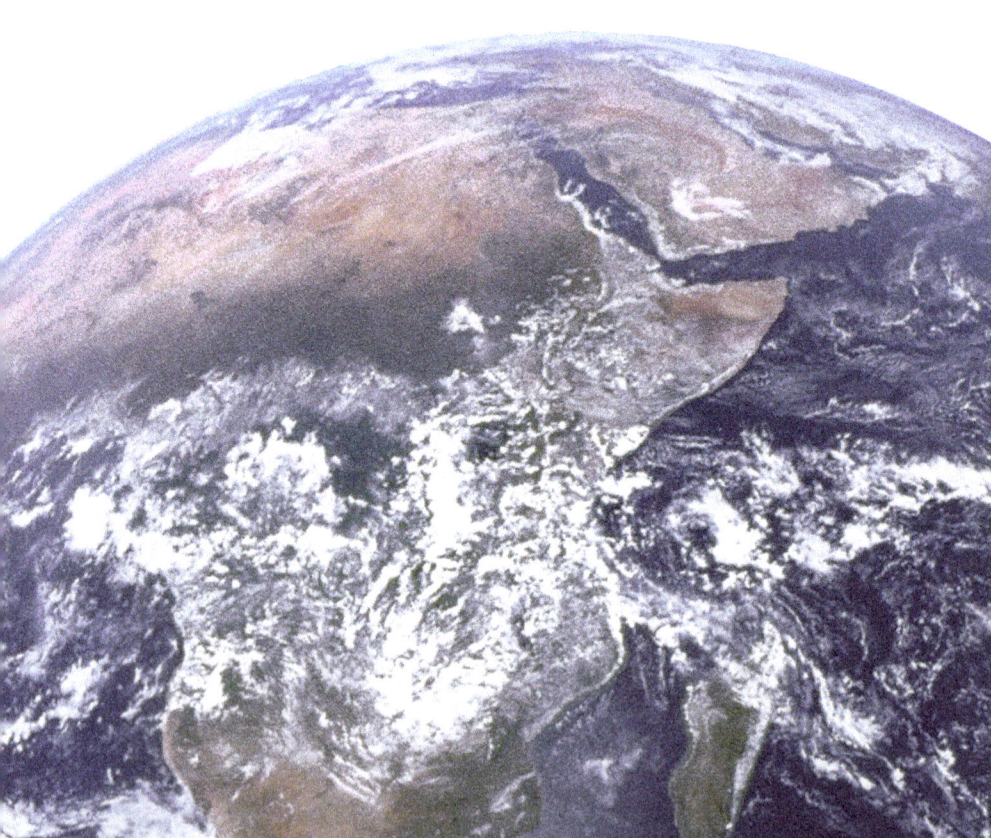

A few centuries ago we woke up to the fact that the world was not flat, but a sphere; and we realized the earth had always been a sphere, even while we had thought it flat.

So now we are awakening to the realization that humanity is one whole society, one global economy, one family of beings in a shared environment.

No matter how cunningly we divide ourselves, between good and evil, or Republican and Democrat, or black and white, or Christian, Muslim and Jew, our divisions are imposed on an already existing unity.

This fundamental condition that we share, the human soul, is unchangeable by religion or government, or by any so-called authority whatsoever.

Our ancestors designed the systems and built the institutions that we've inherited, with each generation modifying the social structure according to the priorities of the time.

When the American colonies threw out the British and constituted a new government, they kept one very important ingredient of British rule, passed down from William the Conqueror, the idea that the ruling power, whether by king or government, wields absolute power over every person, and may force its laws, punishments and wars on all.

In the United States, we're still subject to that power in the form of a national government that recognizes no greater authority than its own, and sustains its power by the compulsory "rule of law."

Each person must submit to an adversarial legal and political system that requires that we struggle with each other for justice, and for power.

We have been taught to struggle as a way of thought, and as a way of life. This condition pervades every aspect of the culture enforced by an absolute authority over all.

Our predicament is that we've inherited a social system that works well for a society of opponents and adversaries. So long as we divide ourselves between friends and enemies, and winners and losers, then the present order of society is workable. However, if our vision is of a more harmonious social order in which human society is perceived as a whole, and in which human conflict is seen as a condition to be avoided, or healed, then the present system won't get us there.

Today we inhabit a new age, a global age, that includes all the races, all the religions and every nation. We are living together here, sharing the same origins, the same conditions and the same destiny, and yet all around the planet we are stuck in the mode of man against man, nation against nation.

Many of us see the absurdity and the tragedy of man against man as a way of life, but feel powerless to intervene. Human self-destruction is sponsored by national governments that recognize no other authority than their own, and condoned by religious institutions that recognize no other morality than their own. None of these governments or institutions serves humanity as a whole, but each pursues its own supposed interests regardless of its effect on the rest of the human family.

There have been radical changes in the human experience over the past few centuries but our governmental, political and legal systems have not kept pace. Our social institutions were designed and built many years ago by warriors for warriors with ideals of dominance, conquest, and defeating the opposition. Now our need is for a new generation of institutions that function for the benefit of the individual person and the whole human family, and in fact, the whole planet.

There is an ancient truth that humanity has known forever but which remains a secret to this civilization. We are directed from a source beyond our reasoning. This source is not in the legislatures, not in the seats of power and not in the temples or churches. It's not outside of us.

The source is within our selves.

We are possessed by an unconscious intelligence that somehow has arranged our moving parts into a living whole, that does what it is doing whether or not we think, whether or not we legislate. This intelligence is the pilot of this life, using the mind as one tool, one sense in a symphony of sensations. This intelligence is at work within each one of us, and throughout humanity.

Just as our individual bodies comprise billions of cells mysteriously unified by the living intelligence into one whole being, so humanity comprises billions of beings mysteriously collected into one whole existence.

We're already connected by this intelligence on wavelengths beyond our reasoning, beyond our wildest dreams.

Our ability to separate ourselves from each other is taking precedence over our connectedness. Our spiritual wholeness is being ignored in favor of ideologies that divide us and keep us apart.

How are we to transcend the organized conflict of man against man?

If we continue to join the conflict, if we pick sides and fight for what we believe and compete for power over others, our personal, social and environmental problems will remain unresolved and we will continue to self-destruct, to suffer.

Man against man is not the answer. Man against man is the problem.

Our quest for a more harmonious social order is not to be achieved by conflict with each other, but by the acceptance of ourselves individually and collectively as a whole. Rather than working against each other, our need is to work with each other.

We can more easily work together for shared benefits than against each other for shared suffering.

If we can free ourselves from the compulsion to struggle, we can then perceive the wholeness of our condition and our inclusion within an already existing unity.

The way we think is within our personal power. The healing of human conflict is an inside job.

By focusing on transactions and relationships where a mutual benefit can be accomplished, where agreement is the goal, the mood of our relationships is transformed. We become creative and caring rather than defensive and greedy. By concentrating on what is mutually beneficial we are happier in our family, and more successful and productive in our community.

Our difficulty is that the requirements of our social order distract us from fulfilling our deepest needs. If the mind is chattering on, hoping for this, fearing that, then any perception of oneself as a whole is excluded.

In order to heal our divided selves we must first notice, then pay complete attention to our inner dialogue, the ongoing chatter of our personal mind. This is the first step on an inward journey.

The inner dialogue reveals our confusion as we try to adapt to the requirements and relationships of an authoritarian and adversarial social system. As we journey beyond the chatter there are hidden emotions waiting to be felt, inhibited hopes and stifled fears waiting to be expressed.

When we allow ourselves to be who we naturally are, to feel our own sensations and love who we love, we are free to contribute our own special talents to the world.

The realization of personal freedom is also the awakening of the soul and the acceptance of who we actually are, rather than who we should be and who we should not be.

The realization is that the self is whole and has always been whole, even while we had thought it divided.

When we dissolve the riddles of our inner world and accept our indivisible selves as a whole without judgment, then the soul can be itself and do its own work for the benefit of the human family. When the mind is rested, and the dualisms are quieted, the awakened person might hear the music of the earth, might step into the eternal moment and realize the absolute freedom of the soul. Such freedom cannot be granted by another, cannot be given or taken away by the rule of law; such freedom cannot be taught or studied or judged, but occurs according to an inner realization unique to the person.

We share a common condition as human beings on Planet Earth. Each of us has a unique path, directed, if we allow ourselves to feel it, by the mysterious intelligence of the living soul within us. This indivisible soul is alive now in its original innocence, here in this place, at this time, being itself, including what we know of ourselves and also what we don't know. Our love, our work, our joyful task is to fulfill the one within. This is the satisfaction we seek. Each of us can do this.

The truths of our existence are beyond governance. No amount of force, no amount of legislation or punishment can solve or remove our differences. Nor will we achieve a more harmonious way of life through revolution, or competitive elections and disputed acts of government.

The truths of our existence are within us and within our personal power.

THAT NOVEMBER MOOD

It all started November 4th, 1968, the night Nixon was elected president. I was walking through the No-Name Bar in Sausalito, a scenic village on San Francisco Bay, following friends to the back patio when, in an instant, as my foot landed on the floor, my life changed. I suddenly realized for the first time that I could do whatever I wanted with my life, and entered a joyous mood, a wide-awake consciousness, that has affected me ever since.

It was as though I had been in a dream, closed off in some inner way, and yet completely unaware of it. Now I was awake and everything was obvious.

I stayed in that blessed mood, freed from any kind of doubt or anxiety for about three weeks, happier and more alive than I had ever been, completely accepting my self and all the selves around me. When the mood left, I did not return to my old self, but was now a seeker, a believer in a new consciousness, and wanted more of it.

In the spring of 1969, Diane and I were joined by Phyllis, who stayed with us for several weeks and became Felicity. After she left I noticed a book she had been reading on the sideboard; it appeared to be by an Indian guru, someone called Krishnamurti.

I had no interest in any kind of guru and the book remained where she had left it. One day, for some unknown reason, I opened the book and read: "You have to find your own way, if you believe in this or that authority, this or that guru, you will never find your own way."

Aha!

I opened the book several times over the next few months and became intrigued by Krishnamurti's point of view and his insights. I would read a page or two and be reminded of that November mood and noticed how my own fears or doubts were in the way.

When, in the summer of that year, Diane and I visited her family in New York, and then my family in England, I brought Krishnamurti's book with me. And then when we impulsively decided to join a group of Australians on an overland journey to India, the book went with us.

Two months later, after an amazing and alarming journey camping across Europe and then most of Central Asia, we arrived in New Delhi exhausted, and collapsed into a modern hotel with showers and clean sheets. The next morning we had an English breakfast of eggs and toast and tea and sat at a table with a South African lady called Joan, and during the conversation she mentioned that later that day she would be attending a talk by Krishnamurti.

So, of course, we went with her and sat expectantly in the large white tent filled with about five hundred people mostly dressed in white. He arrived quietly, also dressed in white, and sat cross-legged on a kind of dais surveying the reverent congregation. He spoke and we listened, but it was not inspiring, and I was surprised to see his hair combed sideways to hide his baldness, and he certainly seemed to be acting like a guru. I was even more critical when after opening the meeting for questions from the audience, he ignored one questioner and then another, and then finally left the stage in a huff. I was amazed. Here was this very rational person, this brilliant thinker, whose book I was carrying around the world, having

a public tantrum for no apparent reason.
I asked Joan, "What was that all about? What just happened?"

"You seem upset," she said.

We walked along the road back towards the hotel and I continued to express my disappointment.

Joan was sympathetic. "If you're very upset, I could possibly arrange for you to discuss it with Krishnaji in person."

"Really?" I said. "That would be great!"

So she made a phone call and I had an appointment.

Later that afternoon I was taken across New Delhi in a bicycle rickshaw to a bungalow on a quiet unpaved street and was greeted by a woman in a sari. She introduced herself as Pupul and offered me tea on the veranda overlooking her beautiful garden.

At last, after tea, she ushered me into a room with two open shuttered windows and furnished with just two chairs, in one of which sat Krishnamurti. I sat in the other chair and we smiled and nodded a silent greeting.

Now, I realized, I have to ask him a question. I felt awkward receiving such special treatment especially since I was more surprised than upset. So I just started to talk. I apologized for taking his time for something trivial but I had come to his talk filled with the expectation of hearing his wisdom in person. I had read one of his books, (brought with me from California), and was impressed with his point of view and his insights into the way the mind works.

"Today," I said, "I was so surprised when, after asking for

questions from the audience, you refused to answer some of them and then abruptly you left the stage apparently angry at the audience."

"Ah, yes," he said. "I was a bit angry then, but I am not now." He laughed.

"You see, some of those people come to all my talks, they follow me wherever I go and ask the same questions; they don't care about the answers, they just want to appear clever. So now I don't answer. But it is annoying. I can't think of any other way to deal with it." He laughed again. "I don't want to encourage them you see."

"Oh," I said, "I see."

We sat silently. He was still smiling. I think I was too. And we sat there in the quiet open-windowed room, waiting for my next question.

I didn't feel like leaving and my mind raced in search of something to fill the silence. At some point I looked at him, and then, my mind just relaxed and I stopped thinking. I don't know how long it lasted but once again I was in that November Mood of acceptance, and he was in it too. In fact he had induced it. So we just sat there being the whole thing, wide-awake on another wavelength than thought.

After a timeless time, I realized that I needed to find a way to experience this feeling of wholeness every day. What was preventing me? Some kind of fear?

I broke the silence. "I think I need to go to a very quiet place for a while to figure out what to do with my life, to let myself flow and see what happens."

"Yes," he said. "Yes, exactly the thing to do."
As I left Krishnamurti and Pupul on the veranda there were tears and a warm current of emotion between us.

The bicycle rickshaw man, Sindhu, was waiting for me at the gate, and as he pedaled me away Krishnamurti waved goodbye with surprising enthusiasm from the veranda.

Something had just happened. My quest for that November Mood had been reinforced, my daily life would now be focused on clearing the way.

> *The ancient wisdom is available to you.*
> *You'll find it on inner wavelengths.*

I spent some time on a mountain top
Got spun around through cold and hot
I listened to my hopes and fears
All through the seasons
All through the years
And on and on it rolls around
I sing my song
As it all rolls on and on.

I built myself a redwood shack
Laughed and cried at what I lacked
Took a journey to my soul within
To where the endings all begin
And on and on it rolls around
We sing our song
As it all rolls on and on.

THE ONENESS

After a small success in society I went around the world and through various cultures, including an overland odyssey from England to India, and returned to California a changed person.

I was no longer willing to play the game of winners and losers, now I needed more from myself.

I moved to an old sheep ranch in the coastal mountains of Northern California, and lived quietly there with my lady, Diane, and the seasons rolled around, and my view of the world changed and I saw deeper into myself.

Then in the sudden silence, I heard the song of the Earth.

We are one, it sang, all of us included.

And then came the news, the old truth I'd been waiting for:

"There is nothing wrong with me!"

I am included in this oneness. I belong here. I am not divisible between good and evil. I am whole. There is nothing wrong with me.

When I visited the city to tell my friends the good news they were aghast. As far as they were concerned I had inexplicably abandoned success and disappeared into the mountains. Now I reappear long-haired and bearded, talking about wholeness. Apparently I had lost it.

They did not get it at all. How could they? Their daily reality was focused on achieving success and wealth and avoiding failure and loss. Life was a struggle between two opposing forces. The idea that these seemingly opposing forces could be one was unthinkable, would lead to certain failure.

In order to survive in our society we are required to be subject to an adversarial legal and political system and to conform to conflicting cultural values. The mad old warrior government insists on battle.

But once you have realized the oneness you cannot unrealize it. Now you know it, you can't unknow it. Now I was stuck in the oneness. How on earth was I going to deal with the twoness of my culture?

One way forward.
No way back.

THE ORACLE

It's time to journey inward, to go beyond a world of our own creation, and to notice the mental defenses we've created to protect ourselves from the hostilities of our social order.

Who am I? What am I doing here?

Let us go then you and I, on a journey within ourselves, and let us start with a purpose:

To uncover the inner secrets of this life…

The journey begins in our mind, where we think we are. Dallying in a labyrinth of our own creation, in a hall of mirrors, debating choices of hope and fear. There on the screen is all that we have ever learned. And there in the corner is the pile of trash, a black hole containing all that we've tried to reject and deny.

Our journey within requires that we find a way out of our mind. We search for an exit. There is none. There is only the trash.

We have no alternative but to enter the trash, that which we have feared… it's the only way out.

Into our own dismal darkness we descend…

There are monsters here, afraid of the light of day, who possess the keys to our fortress. Unknown voices are calling, urging us onward. But the specter of death obscures our view, and now we are pulled helplessly, hopelessly, into death's dark depths, losing gravity, submitting now to what must be, to what is.

Suddenly we awaken, and realize we have entered a new realm.

Behind us the deflated mind now rests as we journey on into the unknown.

Now we are unafraid, and listen to the voices leading us on, as if on a river flowing endlessly, it cannot be stopped. Emotions arise. Passions surge. Must be felt. Love is here, and joy, sadness, and great beauty.

Now we rest within the pulse of the earth. Echoes from the center of the being lead us on and on, alive in the moment, to the beat of the drummer.

As if on a pilgrimage, others arrive. Alone together we climb the magic mountain to see as far as we can see… Ahead of us there are others on the path, behind us too. Voices everywhere.

And then on the far side of the peak, in a cloud of swirling mist, in a protected hollow is the Oracle. The familiar voice speaks:

"Behold the Spirit is your Self. Search no further. What you seek to find you have already! Hone your natural talents to do your special work!"

And the curve of the Earth is all around us. The society of man battles in the distance. The mist swirls, the wind blows, as we descend the traveled path back to where we are recognized and loved.

But knowing now what we've always known. There is a divine thing within us beyond words, which moves us now and evermore.

> *I seek everywhere outside of myself,*
> *before receiving direction from the Oracle,*
> *who points out that the satisfaction*
> *I seek is within myself.*
> *What I seek to find,*
> *I already have.*
> *The understanding awaits my perception.*

*The seed says to the tree: "What am I?"
and the tree says: "You are my seed."*

*And as the seed twists into the earth, the seed says: "Do I belong to you?"
"Yes," says the tree.
"We belong to each other."*

ORIGINAL INNOCENCE

We look to the eyes, to the eyes that see us,
to the face that looms each day.
The mother's face above the crib
smiles and snarls, kisses and barks,
and sings the song of the world.
Pulled as she is by the power outside of her,
she clings to the clutch of her child
and pours into the new-born being
her love for everything
and her fear.

If we retrace our steps along the path that brought us here, we can uncover the original innocence that still exists within us. The so-called sins have been laid on us like cloaks to cover our nakedness. As a child we were subject to the moods and whims of those who protected and provided for us, who covered us with cloaks and exposed us to their fears.

The intelligence within each one of us is a pure thing. Even now, as you read this, no matter how troubled by life, within you is a pure intelligence using your life.

Honor this continuous energy pulsing within you. The original innocence lives on, always available at the untroubled center of your being, alive on myriad wavelengths brought together in you.

Honor this original innocence, the foundation of your life.

Bring it with you. See it in others.

From the center of my being
comes the energy which pushes this pen,
and this center is beyond words,
beyond layers of social
and animal memory,
beyond touch and sound,
beyond silence.

THE LABYRINTH

The intelligence of the whole being is always available, and the original innocence with which we experienced our early years is still accessible.

However, our culture requires of us a vast amount of memory and learned knowledge in order to participate in the way of life. And participation is compulsory. Every child is made to attend school and to be obedient to authority. Disobedience brings punishment and guilt, and the young mind is busied with a learned fear. The 'powers that be' dominate the child and the child learns to divide the whole into right and wrong, good and bad. Therefore as we grow and adapt to the requirements imposed on us, the intelligence of our being is concentrated in our minds by necessity, and our original innocence is obscured and unthinkable.

Let's call this culture with its adversarial rule of law and its absolute authority over the person, with all of its great inventions and its printed money, let's call this way of life: the labyrinth.

The labyrinth includes all that we covet and all that we disdain, a tragic-comic carnival of clowns and monsters, lovers and haters, and winners and losers. In the labyrinth the warrior belief system is in power with rewards and punishments, friends and enemies, persons of power and wealth, and persons in jail waiting to be executed. The labyrinth is a maze of opposites where the challenge to fight the battle is thrust upon us in order to succeed, and in order to survive.

One learns to live with conflict in the labyrinth, adapts to the punishments and strives for the rewards. A person can become skillful in dealing with adversarial relationships like the warrior, the lawyer, and the politician, or one can be obedient and submit to the flow and try to make the best of it.

Many of us feel trapped in the labyrinth and are not well-suited for a life of conflict. We don't want to go to war, or fight legal battles, or run for office; we're much more interested in the pursuit of happiness, or in the enjoyment of nature, or in some artistic endeavor.

We would prefer a more harmonious way of life than the labyrinth can provide.

We'd like to find a way out from the labyrinth but there appears to be none. No exit is permitted. The rule of law is universal and compulsory, as are money, licenses and taxes. The legal and police forces insist on absolute power over each person.

How then, can we contemplate a way out?

The way out is connected to the way in. The way you went in is the way out. By retracing your steps and unraveling the knots you've tied within your mind, by releasing your self from judgment and the confusion of hopes and fears that you were required to learn, you can find your own way out from the labyrinth. The labyrinth is the creation of your mind and does not exist without your thought.

In order to participate in the labyrinth we enter a trance, a dream state, in which we subordinate our selves, our souls, to a power over and outside of us. We suspend our disbelief and submit to the ruling voice. Fooled by fear we wander into the labyrinth doing what's expected of us, just like everyone else.

We can awaken from this trance.

The way out of the labyrinth is by a change in consciousness. When the mind rests, and the chatterer is quiet for a timeless time, the intelligence of the whole being becomes available. When we place ourselves where there is no need for thought, perhaps on a secluded beach or a mountain-top, then, when our thinking stops, we can experience a change in our consciousness - a completely familiar place for each and every one of us. We become aware of a whole intelligence within us that includes all of our processes. This is the indivisible consciousness of the soul.

The soul comes from a place before birth and goes to a place beyond death, and uses the whole brain even as the thinking mind is ignorant of it. As soon as we recognize that the living soul within us is infinitely more aware than our worded sense, the learned values and remembered knowledge can take a lesser place in the being.

When we awaken to the consciousness of the soul we realize that the labyrinth and the warrior belief system is a dream, a creation of the mind, and can be exercised or not, at will. This soul is our original innocence, a whole intelligence in touch with the essence of life itself. The source of life is within us, evolving over millions of years to become this, indivisible, beyond judgment, beyond good and evil, beyond the labyrinth.

There is a guide for you,
one who can lead you out of the labyrinth,
of dualism and the mirrored halls of opposition.
The one who led you in,
can lead you out.
The one who divided the Self
can make the Self whole.
You are the one.

MAKE THE DIVIDED THING WHOLE

What's the message? Make the divided thing whole.

What thing? The social order, the government, the belief system, the self.

Healing the division is the work of the soul.

We've been bamboozled and brainwashed; we've been divided and conquered, we've been enslaved by an illusion, by a false idea.

The self is whole, has always been whole, even as we think it divided. The division is a ruse, a ploy, a deception. The division is a pretense.

So what does this mean? Making the divided thing whole begins within. An acceptance of the whole self heals the division.

The whole self accepts the primacy of the soul and the inclusion of both the conscious and the unconscious intelligence of the whole being.

Occasionally, when the chattering mind is quiet, the soul can emerge into consciousness and the whole human being is awake and available. The soul uses the whole brain. The soul is the indivisible one.

Soul consciousness is our natural state. The awakening from our learned worded consciousness is sometimes known as enlightenment.

Having turned on, we tuned in, then we dropped out.
Now we begin again, and we begin with ourselves.

This self must deal with this society in this world. And human society is a police state.

Okay, I'm free, but that freedom is subject to a ruling power- armed and ready for battle!

How does the free person deal with a police state and the imposed limitations on that freedom?

First and foremost, this is the way things are. This is our condition. The human person is organized into positions of opposition. Each of us has been born into organized human conflict.

So my quest has been to distance myself from the hostilities and to create a way of life that works for me, and provides for my family without harming anyone. I've adapted to the ruler and the powers that be on my own terms, while respecting the person behind the uniform or in the office.

We're all here together and we need to devise a way of life that is not self destructive, that is not divided against itself.

The old ship of state that brought us here is running aground, the crew is divided and the leaders are oblivious to the old ship's condition as they fight for the helm. We watch from afar preparing to build a transitional vessel, a ferry to a fresh start.

The change is within; the worldview changes from within after a cleansing of the conditioned mind and an acceptance of this self.

Can the ship of state be saved? Or do we build a new vessel? Both perhaps.

The first step in saving the ship is to make the divided thing whole.

The person at the helm has the responsibility of the whole ship and everyone on it.

A divided president fighting for control cannot serve the whole population, cannot lead the whole crew, and cannot save the ship.

The presidency must be made whole, beyond party politics, if the ship is to be saved.

Can the adversarial parts yield to the needs of the whole organism? Can we heal the cancer? Can we make our divisive system of governance whole?

The mood of the whole country and even the whole world will change when the U.S. heals its divisive system by instituting a non-partisan presidency.

This can save the ship. It's a first step in making the divided government whole.

Yes to different opinions and diversity; all of it can be heard.

We use agreement as the basis for our games; a common understanding allows us to play the game. So let it be with governance. The agreement cannot be forced. When we founded this nation, we agreed to constitute a government with the consent of the governed. This consent has not yet been realized.

It is the consent that releases us from servitude.

There is however one requirement, one basic understanding we can agree on: This life is sacred.

Our relationships are confused and conflicted by the adversarial system, a system that abuses life. Currently, the child is subjected to a compulsory education stressing that war and human conflict are a constant fact of life.

What would happen if the child were taught that within him or her, there is an intelligent spirit living this life, and this spirit is a consciousness coming from the source?

This spirit exists in each living thing and now we bring it to consciousness. This spirit is sacred. That which you are is sacred.

The life you call your own, the intelligence that moves you, is sacred. No getting away from it.

We've been forced to obey the ruler, to serve the ruler, and therefore we've created a false idea in our mind that this outside ruling power controls our life. This false idea is that we must yield our innate personal power to an inherited and pretended authority. The police power is real but of much less significance than the personal power.

Yes, the world is being run as a police state in which armed force is imposed on every person. What are we to do about this?

We need to return to our roots, to our original innocence, and contemplate the wholeness of it all.

We can discard the false authorities and allow the inner power to bloom.

It's in the consciousness! We all share a common consciousness. Yes the details differ, the rituals are unique, but the ability to understand and to communicate on a shared wavelength is the key because it's the consciousness that joins us.

Making the divided thing whole is a matter of consciousness.

Check it out, we're already whole. One whole planet. One whole human family. One whole person.

At one point we began to divide the whole thing, and we divided it into marvelous inventions. We divided ourselves into nations and religions, and we just kept on dividing and dividing. Now our divisions have multiplied into chaos. Now we are divided against ourselves.

We yearn for a less confusing, less conflicted way of life.

We yearn to make the divided thing whole.

What thing?

The social order, the government, the belief system, the self...

The realization is that the self is whole and has always been whole, even while we had thought it divided.

BOY ON THE BEACH

I've been a boy on the beach but not a man of the sea
The waves keep rolling but I never let them get to me
I've been this way from the start
Spinning through light and dark
I don't know any other way to be.

If you want to know the truth I lied to save my skin
Avoided the bombs of war and kept my secrets in
But then I heard the call of it all
And the sound was coming through me
I turned right around
Stepped into the sound
And went on an inward journey…

I looked through the windows my self to see
And heard all the chatter that belongs to me
Followed the music deep within
Where the endings all begin
There I found a simple thing
I found the old soul within
It's where it has always been.

SOUL CONSCIOUSNESS

We are not centered in our mind, in our identity, we are centered in our soul. The pilot on this voyage is deep within us, and responsible for more than we can think of.

The intelligence of the original seed from which I grew, grows me now.

So, what is this human soul that I am talking about? How do we find it? Where is it?

I am using the word "soul" to describe the whole consciousness that we possess. This whole consciousness includes what we know and also what we don't know - it includes the conscious and the unconscious.

Our mentality can think about a lot of things, but it cannot think about the whole brain, and it cannot think about the whole body. Our thinking is limited, whereas our existence, the actual being that we are, is not limited, and exists far beyond our ability to define it.

The soul is the whole person and the whole being, and this whole being now has a consciousness of the soul. We are now aware of the fact that this presence that we are exists far beyond our measuring, far beyond our judging, and far beyond anyone's evaluation.

So being this is entirely different from thinking this.

The being of the soul exists on multiple wavelengths that the mind cannot recognize or realize. However, we are this soul, we are alive on these wavelengths, and we are here in this universe with enormous powers that our mind cannot perceive. How then, are we to access this whole consciousness, this Soul Consciousness?

We have to make the divided thing whole. Our mind is filled with divisions and judgements. We have to allow our own being to be itself without judgement.

In Soul Consciousness there's no conflict, there are no sides to battle each other, the whole being is indivisible, and the person is a whole condition, even though we can't think about it. So there's another consciousness that enables us to be whole and to consider our presence in a way that is not measurable; that is what I am calling Soul Consciousness.

Our government is based on opposing parts, divided parts, that are in conflict with each other. In fact, these parts are in confusion with each other. In the United States, in Britain, and in the so-called democracies there are parties that divide the whole, and they try to represent a part of the whole, rather than actually dealing with the whole. The president of the United States doesn't represent all the people, he represents one party and takes on positions against various people. This is not a true democracy.

We're evolving towards a true democracy, in which governance depends on the consent of the governed. Our present systems of governmental force, and the adversarial rule of law are not acceptable in a true democracy.

The purpose of governance is not power. The purpose of governance is service. How do we move beyond this divided system? How do we move into a system that represents the wholeness?

The only place we can do that is in our own consciousness. We can look at our own condition, and the condition of the human family as a whole.

The whole condition that we are living is available to us as Soul Consciousness, the consciousness of the whole live being. The human being, after eons of evolution, is here now with all of its capability.

We don't need to "think" about this. We simply need to allow this condition to manifest. We can allow our inner being to be itself, to trust it and to enjoy it, and to be here in a spirit that celebrates our existence on this planet.

Soul Consciousness is our natural state. It's what we are born with, before our mind begins to load up with details, with instructions, with who we have to relate to and how. When we're not thinking, the whole intelligence is available. The ideas that circulate in our culture, the idea that the human being is divided, the idea that we are opposed to each other, and the judgements that linger in our thinking, obstruct the clarity that's available to us with the soul simply being itself.

We don't need to nourish the divided thing, we need to nourish the wholeness. The whole of ourselves. The whole human family. The whole planet.

> *If the Whole is divisible into acceptable and rejectable parts, then such rejectable parts remain included within the Whole.*

Of a cauldron, bubbling, boiling
Nourished by idea
Lives man his life, for all his toiling
For destiny my dear
Yes it breathes and boils and bubbles
Happens all the time
Shaped and moved by all its troubles
Happening now in rhyme.

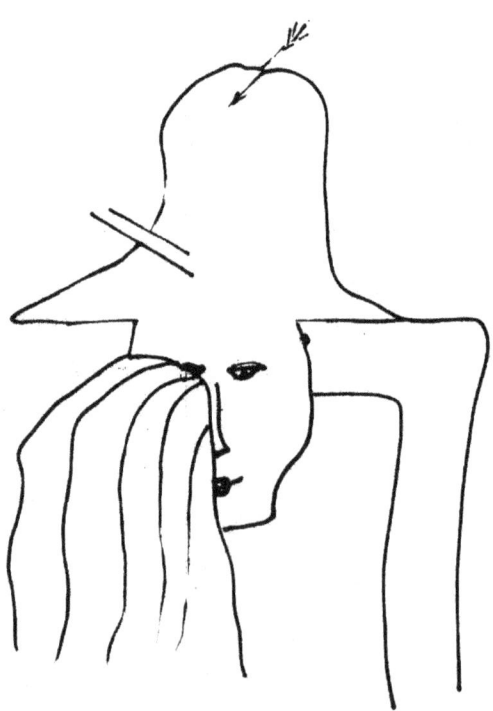

EARLY SORROWS

I was born in London, England just a few years before the second World War. At the age of four, the London Blitz was being launched by Hitler and the German military. Everybody was terrified, and London was on fire. Over 43,000 people died in less than a year of complete and utter destruction.

As a young child, I was very aware of what was happening on a physical level, of seeing the destruction all around me. I remember recognizing the German planes in the sky, and I learned how to draw them. I saw the pilots in the aircrafts, and once I saw a face in a spitfire as it hurtled through Sydenham where we lived.

In the Battle of Britain, the British were defending London from the German Luftwaffe (the German air force), and the battle was fought by the young British pilots and their incredible machines - the spitfires and the hurricanes. These fighter planes were very quick, and they could out-maneuver the German aircraft. The Battle of Britain was the Germans against the British, in the sky above southern England.

We all witnessed it, and we all suffered it.

Eventually, the Germans gave up and retreated to France. I remember Churchill speaking on the radio about the young fighter pilots, "Never has so much been owed by so many, to so few."

As a boy, I don't remember being afraid. I was very aware of the tragedy and the suffering that the people around me were going through, including my mother, my father, and my uncle. They certainly didn't want to go to war, but they had to because England was being attacked and it was compulsory. If you didn't go to war you went to jail, or some kind of ignominious future. So my father joined up in the air force, and my uncle joined up in the army.

My view of all this, was that we needed to stop those German planes, and to defeat Germany. We had to find Hitler and kill him. That was essential, because this was all springing from one mad brain that was enlisting all these Germans into an outrageous war. I remember standing in the road once, pretending to shoot down a Messerschmitt bomber, when a man came up and pushed me out of the way and told me to get to the bomb shelter. I was a witness to the destruction.

I hated the Germans. I hated Hitler. I was terrified that my father and uncle would be killed. My uncle did get killed in the last year of the war.

London also suffered another form of attack from the Germans, and that was from pilotless aircrafts, the V1s and the V2s. V1s were the buzzbombs, and the V2s were rockets. The buzzbombs were loaded with incendiary bombs to start fires, and they were filled with enough fuel to get them somewhere around the Thames River in London. I would wake up in bed and hear the drone of the buzzbomb, and the drone would suddenly stop, and when it stopped, you knew it was descending. The fact that you heard it stop meant that it was really close. So we had this ominous interlude, from the stopping of the buzzbomb's engine, to the explosion that happened very soon afterwards. This was the most terrifying period of time.

My family's house was partly destroyed earlier in the Blitz, and we moved to an apartment where we were on the fourth floor, and as a kid, I could see all over South London. I could see all the fires and people being killed, and it was just weird. It was a feeling of rot, of nastiness, and of dysfunction.

Surprisingly, the war ended. The British and the Americans after D-Day waltzed, with huge bloodshed, through France, Belgium, and Holland and then entered Germany. My uncle was killed as the British army crossed the Rhine River. This brought enormous suffering to our family.

When the war ended everything changed, and it was an unexpected feeling for me. Even though the war was over, I still hated the Germans. All the death and destruction that they caused was still in me, and shortly after the war ended the strangest thing happened.

German prisoners of war, in dungarees and outfits that had "P.O.W." written on their backs, were walking around Sydenham, my small town which was part of South London, and as they walked around, I was seething.

"What on earth?! Why are we letting these Germans walk around, when they've just done what they've done?!"

I saw this German prisoner in particular, with blonde hair, who looked right at me. I wasn't afraid of him, but there was something that I felt that I couldn't explain. It was a dark deathly feeling. I saw him three times, and on the third time,

I was standing on the other side of the street. I looked at him and he looked back at me with a kind of half-smile. He looked okay, he wasn't ferocious or upset or anything, and it actually seemed like he was trying to be nice. I walked over to him and I really let him have it.

"You Germans have been awful! You have killed so many people that you didn't even know, and we had to hide from you every night! It was a disaster! Why did you do it?! What did you get out of it?! Now that you've lost the war, what did you get out of it?!"

As we walked past the bombed-out buildings on Kirkdale Road, he could barely answer any of my questions because he knew little English, but my verbal deliberation and determination was sufficient for him to understand what I was saying. At last, he said something to me that really impacted my whole life. He said he didn't know anybody in the prisoner of war camp, or anyone else in Germany, that wanted to go to war. Nobody wanted it. It was forced on them, and if they refused they were punished with concentration camps, or even being killed.

I am standing there listening to this, in amazement. What kind of life is that? What is that about? What kind of people are these Germans? And then I thought about my father, and my uncle who had just been killed. They didn't want to be in the war. What's going on?

How come wars are being fought, and hardly anybody wants to be in them?

This question has stayed with me, and has become a focus for a lot of my work. The idea of dividing ourselves between friend and enemy, and then killing each other is absolutely insane.

The point is to create a better way of life than dividing ourselves into friends and enemies, good and evil.

The point is to create a more harmonious way of life than we've inherited.

We can more easily work together for shared benefits, than against each other for shared suffering.

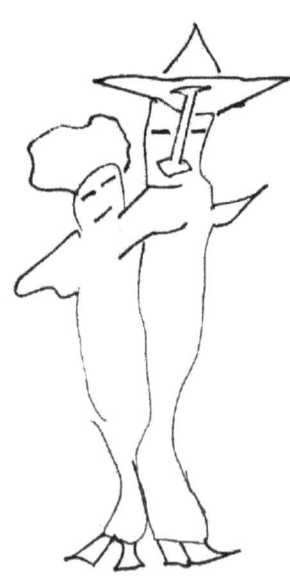

THE INWARD JOURNEY

You've been conditioned, trained and educated, to believe in a greater power than your own, a vast presence, an almighty God, an all-powerful authority, somewhere out there, an outside power beyond your reach.

The outside power is a false authority, a device of subjection. You no longer need it.

I'm asking you to look within, because within you is your own access to the universal intelligence that runs the show.

You are the living truth, already in touch with the source of it all.

The inner power, the ultimate freedom, awaits your perception.

Go there.

Take the inward journey to your soul.

After going around the world and experiencing several different cultures, and after spending time with Krishnamurti, and having that November Mood confirmed, I went to a new environment. I moved to a beautiful ranch of 280 acres, in the coast mountains of Northern California. I moved there with my lovely wife, Diane, and went on the inward journey of exploring my own being.

What am I doing with this life? What do I want to do?

I knew I could make money by working hard in the real estate business. But money was not it. Money was a fuel, something that was going to help, but the real question was: what is my purpose and what am I here to do? And I didn't know.

So Diane and I moved into this isolated place with forest, meadows and mountains. We were in a kind of seclusion. We had a good library of books, but we had no electricity, except what we created with a generator. We went into this quiet existence, where I was exploring my inner being. I also probed the depths of my psyche through the use of LSD.

I had taken LSD and became aware that there was a fear lingering within me. It felt like a fear of death, of something that I couldn't quite embrace, that I was avoiding. And so it became a motive for me to go into this fear. I had to find this fear and fully experience it, and see it clearly for what it was.

So one day in June, I took LSD again and went out into a quiet meadow, took off all of my clothes, and faced the whole thing. I tried to fathom what was going on within me.

Suddenly I heard the drone of a plane above me. This sound triggered a huge response: I was panicking, I was tense, I felt threatened. I realized at the same time as I was feeling threatened that it didn't' make sense for me to have this fear. It did make sense for the boy to have the fear, because the fear was necessary for survival. I had to get out of the way of the bombs, and I had to be in a protected place. But now, here I am, a man of 33 in the coast mountains of Northern California, and this is just a private plane, and I don't need this fear. This fear came from my experience of the war. It had been with me ever since, and it was a legitimate fear.

The boy needed the fear. But now, I didn't need it, so I let it go. I breathed out, and it went out from me. And as the fear left me, I suddenly started to cry, and then to sob. The sobbing got heavier, and it became apparent that I was releasing something from deep within me. It was an absolutely powerful feeling. I was witnessing it as it occurred, and it was an intensely visceral event. My mind, the thinker, was looking at it in awe, questioning how this could be happening to me. The sobbing went on and on.

I was kneeling in a meadow of dried grasses, and slowly as the sobbing winds down, I begin to hear music, and it's beautiful. I don't know what it is, I think it might be Mozart, or something. Certainly it had to be something I've heard before, but it was unbelievably beautiful, and I was able to sing along with it. I went up to the farmhouse and sang it for Diane. I asked her "What is this? Where is it coming from?" She said, "It's so beautiful, but I've never heard it before."

From that moment, in that cleansed state, I began to hear music, and the music seemed to be a part of my own history, it seemed to come from deep within me. There were deep emotions in the tones, and these tones carried so much meaning for me. They filled me with ecstasy, with deep love.

The childhood fear has gone, and here comes the music.

Wow.

The music was mysterious and wonderful. I bought a piano right away and began to listen for the tones that I wanted to hear. And in this whole experience was the sensation of what I call the "November Mood." The consciousness of being aware of those tones, of actually listening to them and being them, was in fact the same consciousness that I had experienced of acceptance, of complete allowance of my own inner being to be itself. Not editing it, and not changing it, but being it. The music was exactly this. The music was what now I could rest in, and with it came the continuation of the inward journey into my purpose and what I wanted from this life.

What I wanted was a peaceful life. I wanted to be comfortable, relaxed, and unafraid. I was able to create this at the farm. I created a place where people could live harmoniously with an understanding of what this life is about. It was not about being a threat against anybody, and we were not using force of any kind. We could be open to being on this planet, in this beautiful environment where we had put ourselves, and of going towards what we actually wanted. All of this was possible at the farm. We had an environment where there was a lot of sensible philosophy, a lot of allowance of each other, and no real imposition of rules or regulations. In this environment, I learned a lot about how to work with others to our mutual benefit.

I had accomplished the quest of the inward journey, of cleansing my inner being of my fears. My life was now up to me. I had nothing to be afraid of, nothing to run away from.

It was now a matter of encountering the whole thing. And the whole thing was within me.

EARLY MORNING, GREY AND STILL...

Early morning grey and still, my ears digest the sounds around me: the frogs, the bleating goats, the ravens cawing, the rush of the stream in the woods, the burning of the fire in the stove, the tweet and the rasp of unknown beings around me. Busy busy place, all of it happening together. Most of the time I am unconscious of my participation in a gigantic happening; I live inside my own sounds listening to the chatter of my mind. Or I am making my own noise, the noise of man, talking, roaring, hammering, busy inside the making of my life. But sometimes my thinking and my doing stop; and I am still, and I am alive through the amazing awareness of my senses without thought or action - holding as t'were a mirror up to nature - seeing into the very life of things - witnessing "the kingdom of heaven."

The ideals of man's religions have been constructed in order to facilitate the seeing into the life of things, informing the believers of another state of consciousness in which anxiety and pain were not. The religious ideal is always a political weapon; the concept of one who seeks power. The man who spends his life climbing the hierarchy of a church is no different from the man who spends his life climbing the hierarchy of a bank. Each requires acknowledgement of authority and therefore trust in the system. Each is involved with maintaining a morality. Each seeks power, the same power he is afraid of. And he seeks power as a result of absorbing and believing a religious ideal.

The religious ideal is the kingdom of heaven, paradise, release from guilt and suffering, success and triumph; all of which derive from misunderstanding the tales of those men who have been a reflection of nature, who have seen into the life of things and tried to tell about it. There are those who experience the kingdom of heaven whose lives are absorbed in the discovery of what is happening, in the interdependence of all things. And there are those who believe they are inadequate, incapable of experiencing the kingdom of heaven; that they are sinful and unfortunate; who strive towards the ideal of their absolution and acceptance.

There are a few great men. A great man is one who lives in harmony with the way of the earth, who refuses to accept the division of man between good and evil, friend and foe. The great man experiences his own reality. He neither feels nor perceives authority. His concern is with the inevitability of what is. He lives through his own senses, his own mind. He accepts the being that he is and glories in it. His mind is in touch with the unknown. For man he faces the outside; but for himself he lives nourishing his own body, sustaining his own existence. For this is true selflessness: that he treats himself as humanity.

There is no one way to the kingdom of heaven. You will spend your senses as you wish. No authority can show you the way to your satisfaction. Each one of us is alone within a downy skin possessed of our senses and a mind to catalogue our experiences. We live alone pursuing our own benefits.

The kingdom of heaven was Christ's trip. He liked to get high. Whenever he wasn't high he talked about the kingdom of heaven as an idea, a good place to be. And he tried to communicate what it was like and how to get there. The kingdom of heaven was an idea from Christ's mind. Those who have not understood the meaning of Christ believe in the kingdom of heaven as an ideal state of mind. The perpetuation of the ideal is the achievement of those who understand neither Christ nor themselves. The ideal was salvaged from the wreckage of Christ's life as the thing he believed in - his ideal. By adopting a stance close to Christ those who studied him attempted to absorb some of his power, and created from the ideal of his words the authority of their lives.

So authority is the device of those who fear they have no power, who have already accepted a power over themselves. Authority is the overcoming of evil and wrongness by those who suffer from evil and wrongness. Authority is the absence

of true leadership. The great man leads, going his own way, unconscious, mindless of who might follow, devoting his attention to where he is going. This is why he is easy to follow, because he is coordinated and going his own way.

There's nothing more frightening than following when you don't know where you're going. He who faces his followers, fears his followers and is possessed by them. He who is busy with his song must be free from followers; his song is to be heard, not to be praised or followed, criticized or denied. The song of man is within each of us. We recognize it as of ourselves when we hear it.

He who points the way
Knows not the way
He who knows the way
Now goes the way

What's to be done?
I say to the sun,
My life has begun to please me.

THE INTELLIGENCE

We've been talking about a change in consciousness.

What is this change of consciousness?

The change we're going through, is an evolutionary change based on the structure of our social order, and how we are required to conform to it.

The old power of the king was absolute over everyone in his kingdom, and now in the nation, there is an absolute power, usually in the government, but sometimes in a dictator or in an authoritarian regime, and the power is imposed on the whole population. We have an authoritarian and tyrannical situation all around the world. Every single government insists on absolute power over all of its citizens. Every person that grows up in this world, who receives an education and training, is required to be obedient to this outside power. This authority, whether it be called king, president, or God, is a power outside of the self.

We have been living according to this outside power for centuries, and we now have a world of nation states, in which the only power that any of these nation states will honor, is their own. This belief, that we're all trained to accept, this teaching that the power is outside of us, this understanding that we are just little beings of no great consequence, that we must be obedient to this outside power and conform to its requirements - this understanding is now changing.

We are waking up to the realization that the power is not outside of ourselves, the power is actually within us. It's not on a throne, it's not up in the sky, it's actually deeply within our own being. We are rooted in this universe, and the intelligence that brought us here, that is still with us, is the intelligence of the universe. What else could it be?

Now this transition from being obedient to a power outside of ourselves, to fulfilling the actual power within us, is what we are now engaged in. Now we recognize the power is within the person, in fact it's within the consciousness.

We want to fulfill this life we are living. We want to be this energy, this love, this whole person to its fullest extent, to be awake and alive on this planet, and to be contributing our energy to something that works.

We want a more harmonious way of life than we've inherited.

The idea of being ruled, dominated, and forced into wars and conflicts is now passing. We now want to live harmoniously in our world, in our own space, interdependent with others and in love with the life being lived, without feeling enslaved by an antiquated social order.

So we awaken now, we move forward now, with our own individuated being in charge of this life. We are not subject or enslaved to an outside power. We are ruled by the intelligence within us.

We are possessed by an intelligence which recognizes no master.

On Earth I sit,
at peace with it,
as the glorious golden orb
is swallowed by the sea.

THE INNER PERSON

The inner person is our priority, not the outside authority, not the judge, not the commander-in-chief, nor the medical expert. The treatment is from within. Even the madman murderer must be understood by himself before change is possible.

Murdering the murderer continues the madness.

The path of each person is valid. Each living thing is on its own course moved by an inner intelligence. If we can honor this intelligence within each person, our conflicts and self-destructive behavior will be diminished.

The only vehicle we have is the person, nothing less, nothing more. "The People" is an idea in the mind of a person.

If we are to devise a more harmonious way of life it must benefit the person. We are all here together, a particular species, evolving through birth and death on this spinning orb, which even now is zipping through the heavens with all of us aboard. Although we may not realize it, we are in fact sharing this Earth, and totally contained within it.

What are we doing here? What's going on?

If we could watch a time-lapse film of the planet over the past century, we would see huge cities erupting with an accelerating humanity, great chains of mechanized energy and newborn billions of people suddenly rushing around the world. We would see wars like cancers on the body of humanity, a global skin disease of human self-destruction, exploding before our eyes.

What is this strange disease we suffer that destroys our lives? What kind of confusion is it that sets person against person and nation against nation, not just in argument but with atrocities to the death? Why can't the children of Abraham share their resources and work together for their mutual benefit? Why do we habitually choose to kill and maim each other? Is this the same confusion that sets the cells of the human body against each other?

We say of course that a healthy human body does not have cancer, but do we say that a healthy human society does not have wars?

Not yet. We're still defending ourselves with a vengeance.

> *Vengeance against the person is not to the benefit of the community. And vengeance by the community is not to the benefit of the person.*

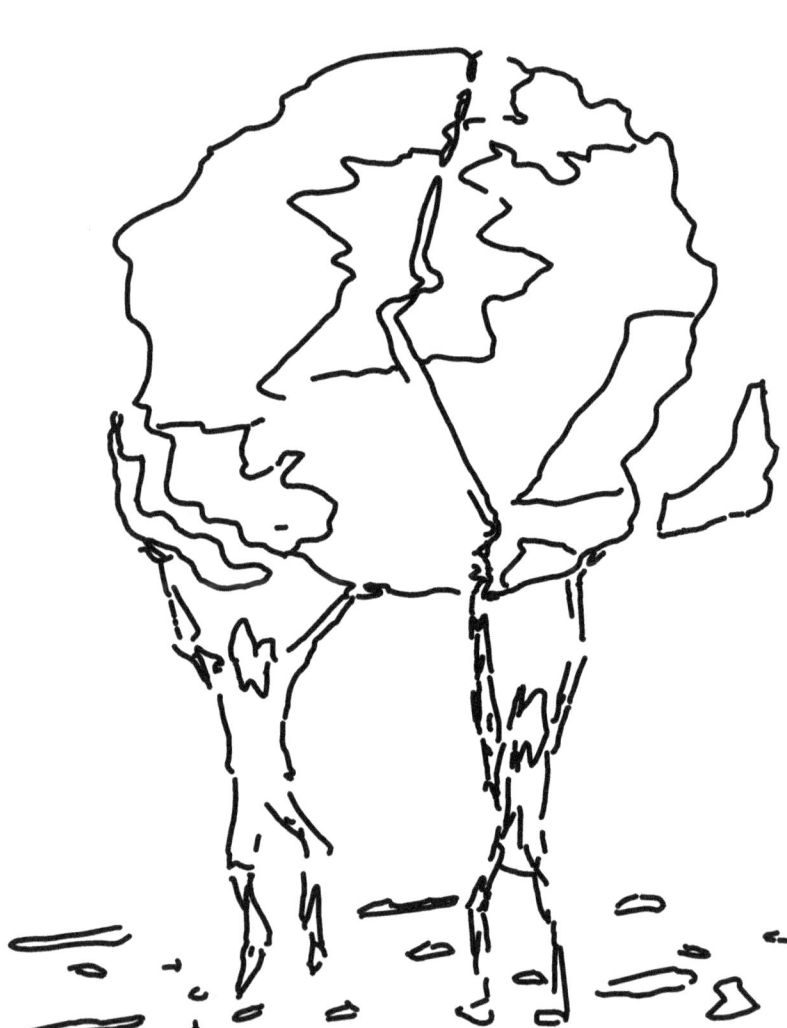

THE GAME IS UP

Since man killing man became a way of life, and people killing people became big business, government has cornered the market. Only men and women authorized by government are allowed to be killers, otherwise killing is a crime punishable by death, executed by a government authorized killer. Government is in absolute power and each person is its subject.

When the British Parliament beheaded Charles the First in 1640, they took away the power of the King, the absolute power over the people inherited from William the Conqueror, and retained it for themselves. And when the American colonies declared their independence from Britain, and constituted a new government, they too retained the inherited power of the conqueror to rule and regulate the people.

The original idea behind the Declaration of Independence was to create a democracy of free and equal people, with the consent of the governed, unfettered by any form of tyranny. We're not there yet. We are still subject to the power of the conqueror in the form of a ruling government that recognizes no greater authority than itself.

The whole human family is subject to the policies and the vision of the United States government. The vision is of a world at war.

This is not the vision of the American people whose sons and daughters are sacrificed. This is the vision of American and international special interests, mega-corporations, arms manufacturers, oil companies, motivated by greed for power and wealth. These special interests pay for the election campaigns of the president. It's no surprise therefore that these investors in the president can influence his policies. These same backers invest in both candidates for president, and in both political parties, thereby guaranteeing their influence in the government no matter who wins election.

Is this any way to run a country? Do we consent to this?

We have not yet achieved a democracy of free people. The consent of the governed has not yet been realized.

The United States and Britain have adopted a system of Adversarial Democracy, sponsored by big business, incorporating conflict between citizens, and war between nations, into an organized way of life.

Since law and politics rule the nation, and the law and the politics are adversarial, then we can expect the lawyers and the politicians to be skilled in adversarial relationship, and we can expect the culture to be in a constant state of war.

In addition to the foreign wars in Korea, Vietnam, the Persian Gulf, the Balkans, the Middle East, Afghanistan, Iraq and Syria, we've had the war on drugs, the war on poverty, the war on crime, now we have the war on terrorism, which is to say war everywhere, all the time. Ironically the more we war against drugs, poverty, crime, the more they flourish. The war on terrorism will sponsor more terrorism.

Is this what we want?

> *"It's no measure of health to be well adjusted to a profoundly sick society."*
> — *Krishnamurti*

The destruction of the World Trade Center was a crime against humanity. People of all races, religions and nationalities were murdered on September 11th, 2001. This mad act of human self-destruction occurred in a world marketplace for the whole human family to witness. It symbolizes the desperate confusion of our condition.

The bombing of people by people, no matter how smart or crude the device, whether sanctioned by Osama bin Laden or the U.S. President, whether it's the World Trade Center, or Oklahoma City, or a Bali night club, or Belgrade, or Baghdad, or it's poor Afghanistan, the bombing of people by people harms all of us.

Who said we shouldn't kill each other?

Was it a Christian? A believer in Islam? Was he Jewish?

The manufacture and distribution of weapons of human self-destruction is out of control.

Humanity has been growing and escalating its power to self-destruct for millennia. From the tribal skirmishes of our remote ancestors to the whole world at war, we have come to the moment where change is imperative.

The game is up!

> *"Our scientific power has outrun our spiritual power. We have guided missiles and misguided men."*
> — *Martin Luther King*

To uncover your personal power and the purpose of your soul, go to a quiet place where you can be fearless and hopeless for a timeless time, and wait for nothing to happen.

IT'S NOT OUT THERE, IT'S IN HERE

All around the world we now have government by armed forces in power over the individual person. The consent of the governed is neither considered nor realized.

The so-called sovereignty of the nation is not of benefit to the individual person nor the whole human family, it allows corrupt regimes to commit atrocities, and allows civil wars to continue unabated. It also ignores human suffering, and in fact exacerbates it.

If our objective is personal freedom in a peaceful world, it won't be possible in a world of sovereign nations.

Wars rage across the Middle East and Africa. Millions of Syrians and Iraqis seek asylum having abandoned their homes, their lives in ruins.

The so-called "rulers" of the so-called "sovereign nations", and the terrorists they oppose, aggravate the human wound by blindly bombing defenseless human beings.

Much of the human family is armed and ready for battle in a trance of self-destruction, a trance in which innocent people kill innocent people for no reason, a trance based on a colossal misunderstanding of what this life is all about.

How do we awaken from this trance of human conflict as a forced fact of life? How do we open the human mind to a fresh understanding of what this life is about?

How about a change of mind?

A change of mind means a change of purpose.

If our purpose is to experience a more harmonious way of life than we've inherited, if we're looking for our personal freedom in a peaceful world, we can do it. We can change our mind.

We've been trained and conditioned since early childhood to be obedient to authority; we were steeped in compulsions and punishments, and we did as we were told.

However, there are two kinds of authority: the one that uses force to sustain its power, and the one we consent to. The rulers' dictates and enforcements, the jealous and vengeful gods, are not in power over us. The true power is not outside of us.

The power, the truth, the freedom, is within. Not out there. In here. The change of mind is to place the emphasis of this life where it belongs, within. Not out there. In here.

This simple change enables an evolving worldview to emerge. We are becoming one human family in one earthly environment and the outside powers, the sovereign nations, and the various religions, their laws and their dogma, can assume a lesser place in the personal mind.

Our change of mind places responsibility for this life on the one living it. The emphasis now is personal, instinctual and intuitive, beyond the reach of invented entities. We want a harmonious way of life and a peaceful world. We can be harmonious on purpose. This is a personal responsibility. It's not out there. It's in here.

Is it true that among the trees
A way is traveling on the breeze
Of how to live and how to grow
Of all that any tree should know.

EVOLUTIONARY EVENT

An evolutionary event is occurring, and it's within each one of us. We are returning to our source, allowing our inner truth to be refreshed with a new understanding. Our understanding of what this life is about is not fixed by teachings, laws, or money. The outside powers that divide us and enslave us with rewards and punishments can move over now. Now we awaken to find that the ruling authority is running amok and the person is enslaved to a conflicted way of life.

The new understanding requires neither dominance, nor submission. The new understanding is to fulfill the life being lived, without harming others. Each of us can do this. Each soul wakes up and sees a purpose - to fulfill the life being lived. An ancient truth can now be brought forth from within. The oneness of our condition, as self, as society, and as planet, is now apparent to the human intelligence.

> *We have entered a New Age, a Global Age, in which our consciousness, our attitudes and systems of relationship are adapting to our newly discovered awareness of ourselves as one species on one whole planet.*

RENAISSANCE

A rebirth of the human spirit is underway.

Our objective is a more harmonious way of life than we've inherited. After many centuries of obedience to the ruling governmental and religious authorities, the time has come to return to the inner truth and empower ourselves from within. This doesn't require conflict with the so-called authorities; they continue to exist whether or not we empower them. The personal power comes from the soul within, no matter what the teaching.

We need to make our systems whole, to heal the inherited divisions with a fresh worldview and a new story of what we're doing here together. We can now build anew from the ground up, a new structure of human relationship in which personal freedom is implicit. Personal freedom leads to personal responsibility and to the possibility of a true democracy in which government is not set against the person. The purpose of democratic government is not power, the purpose of a democratic government is service, for everyone.

The sovereignty of the king yielded to the sovereignty of the nation, now the sovereignty of the nation yields to the sovereignty of the person.

All around the world an ancient understanding is reborn. This life is sacred. Once confined to the tribe, the ancient truth now applies to the whole human presence on this ever-changing planet. This life is sacred.

We are one human family.

We are not ruled by governments or tyrants. We are ruled by the living intelligence within us, and this intelligence has no master.

The source of the life energy and the truths of our existence are within our personal power, and happening now.

We want a peaceful world and a more harmonious human family. Let's make it happen.

Let's be harmonious on purpose.

One person at a time…

Pale Blue Day
Listen as I say
Once more in words
I found the way

Let no person demand as a right that which he will not accord to others.

FORBIDDEN JOURNEY

I had to take a long forbidden journey
Far beyond all sense of right and wrong
Where no-one could lead me or follow me
I had to go there alone.

Underneath the ground through city subways
All around the world I flew the sky
In nightclubs, on beaches, and boulevards
Rushing through day and through night.

I walked into Sotheby's and heard a voice in my ear
"They've gone beyond the limit," she said. "We'd better get out of here!"
The man on the wall looked down on us all
And the music began in my head
And the song that I sing came out of me that night in bed.

Everywhere I went I heard the music
Seemed like a song from long ago
A singer was singing the melody
The voice that I heard was my own.

I went to a simple mountain top and breathed the living air
I looked at the birds and trees and things until there was nothing there
And then in the sudden silence
I awoke from the dream
And the man on the wall was gone
And I knew that I was free.

It's not about a hero for the story
It's not about the maestro who would teach
The wisdom was buried inside of me
Here within my reach.

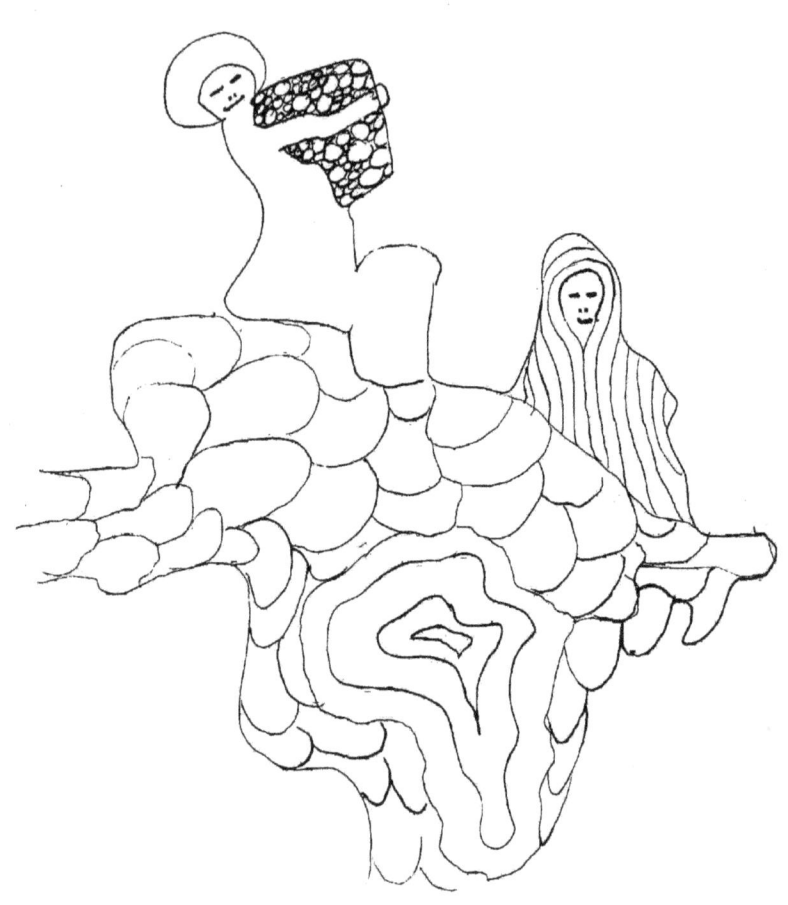

THE CAGE

Not far from here there is a cage, with hundreds of unhappy people locked inside. Outside the cage armed guards are watching. A boy is trying to squeeze out through the bars of the cage. The boy's mother is embarrassed as people around her snarl angrily. She pulls him back and scolds him.

"If you go out there, bad things will happen," she says. "You could die!"

Again and again he tries to escape. Again and again she scolds him.

Then, one night when the moon is full and everyone is sleeping, the boy sucks in his breath… He squeezes and squeezes, and the bars seem to bend. He's almost through… suddenly he's outside the cage!

He pauses. No-one has noticed.

A guard lies snoring next to the gate. He is chained to the cage. The boy notices the key to the cage is around the guard's neck, he runs into the woods. He's free!

When he is far away from the cage he climbs a tree and rests.

Over the next months the boy learns to take care of himself by helping others. He helps a farmer during harvest, and a shepherd with his sheep. And he grows bigger and stronger.

Every day he thinks of his mother and all the unhappy people trapped inside the cage. He resolves to set them free.

One day he sets off on a journey back to the cage. He arrives at night while the guards are sleeping. Carefully he takes the key from around the guard's neck, and unlocks the gate of the cage. He finds his mother and gently wakes her up.

"Quick!" He says to his mother. "Let's go! The gate is unlocked and I have the key." She is horrified and angrily refuses to leave.

"Come on," he says to the unhappy people. "You're all free!"

The people stare back at him and grumble. No-one wants to leave the cage.

So, taking the key with him, and leaving the gate unlocked, he leaves the cage once more, disappointed and sad to leave his mother behind, but now that he's found his freedom he will never let it go.

A soft rain is falling as he runs through the woods to the open fields beyond.

> *"I know where I'm going and I know the truth, and I don't have to be what you want me to be. I'm free to be what I want."*
> — *Muhammad Ali*

OUT FROM THE DARKNESS OF A CONQUERED LIFE

What about the kingdom of heaven? The kingdom of heaven is a wavelength accessible by the living person when the mind is open.

The rich man can't access the kingdom of heaven while protecting his wealth. The citizen's concerns about legal and illegal, about profit and loss, are laid like a screen over the soul's presence and the kingdom of heaven is obscured.

The hidden path to the soul can be uncovered, the feelings revealed, the lover unmasked, the kingdom of heaven experienced.

The aperture through which the soul can be revealed is the open mind.

If you're looking for your soul, with what are you looking?

Each person is a living soul, on a particular path, out from the darkness of a conquered life, seeking fulfillment.

Who would doubt it?

THE THREE STEPS

You've got to want to do what you're doing, before you can do what you want.

There are three steps each of us can take that will enable us to transcend the adversarial quagmire:

> 1. Recognize and admit that you can spend your life as you wish. You are choosing your own path and you are responsible for your own personal fulfillment.

> 2. Acknowledge the given talents that you are blessed with, and develop your natural abilities into skills. Become skillful at what you love to do.

> 3. Now use those developed skills to work with others for your mutual benefit, without harming anyone. Focus on a mutual benefit in all relationships and all transactions.

Billions of us want a peaceful world and a more harmonious human family.

We can make it happen.

One person at a time...

"And the day came when the risk it took to remain tight inside the bud was more painful than the risk it took to blossom."

– Anais Nin

A NEW STORY

Our civilization is in the process of a great change. We're going through a change in the mythic story of the culture, from one understanding of our condition to another. A new story is arriving.

The old story is that we are in a dualistic world, divided between good and evil, and friends and enemies. We have been taught and conditioned by a divisive and adversarial belief system that insists on conflict as fundamental to the human condition. Also, we've inherited a way of life that is predicated on the dominance of a ruling authority that is armed and ready for battle. The old story is of wars and massacres, of human self-destruction as a fact of life, and it continues to this day.

But now a new story is emerging that reflects changes in our condition. As the old story has divided humanity the new story is concerned with the wholeness of our condition and a more harmonious and inclusive worldview.

Many will say change is impossible, that human conflict is inevitable. We've been raised on a history of war and conquest and heroism in battle. This is the way we are.

No doubt this is the way we have been, and continue to be. However, we are evolving and the increased awareness of our planetary condition, of being one human species in one earthly environment, creates a fresh perspective of what we're doing here.

The new story is about a worldview we can all live with.

War has erupted again in the Middle East and the children of Abraham are inflicting death and suffering on each other, as the world looks on, horrified and seemingly powerless to intervene. The great religions at the root of the conflict insist on separation and divisiveness with each other and generally refuse to get along, notwithstanding their shared roots.

Can the children of Abraham awaken to a fresh vision of the ancient truth we've always known? Each of us, and each living thing, is in direct contact with the universal source of life, call it Allah or Yahweh or God. This direct connection within us is sacred, and beyond the reach of divisive ideologies, or any authority whatsoever.

Can we accept this sacred quality in each other? Can we accept this inner freedom, this sovereignty, and at the same time recognize that our world has changed since the ancient texts were written?

We are no longer isolated tribes in an uncharted world. We are one human family in one earthly environment. Our condition and our awareness is now global.

The old story doesn't work for humanity as a whole, nor is it concerned with the whole planet. It wasn't created with a whole planet in mind. We have inherited divisive systems and customs that were designed for another time that are now no longer appropriate or beneficial.

Can we awaken to a global vision, including all the tribes, all the nations, and all the religions, and recognize that we need a more harmonious way of life on this planet? Can we disentangle ourselves from the obsolete divisions that are causing intolerable human suffering, and unchain ourselves from the perpetual unforgiving vengeance? Can we honor the sacred source within each one of us?

Yes we can.

One person at a time.

As our culture reveals its instability, its corruption and self-destructive confusion, the power of the authorities is losing presence in the personal mind and the focus goes inward, returns to the self, and ultimately to the soul.

How do we apply the new story? We create a harmonious life in the adversarial culture.

We begin again.

One person at a time.

I am one.

My family is one.
My tribe is one.
My nation is one.
My world is one.

I am one.

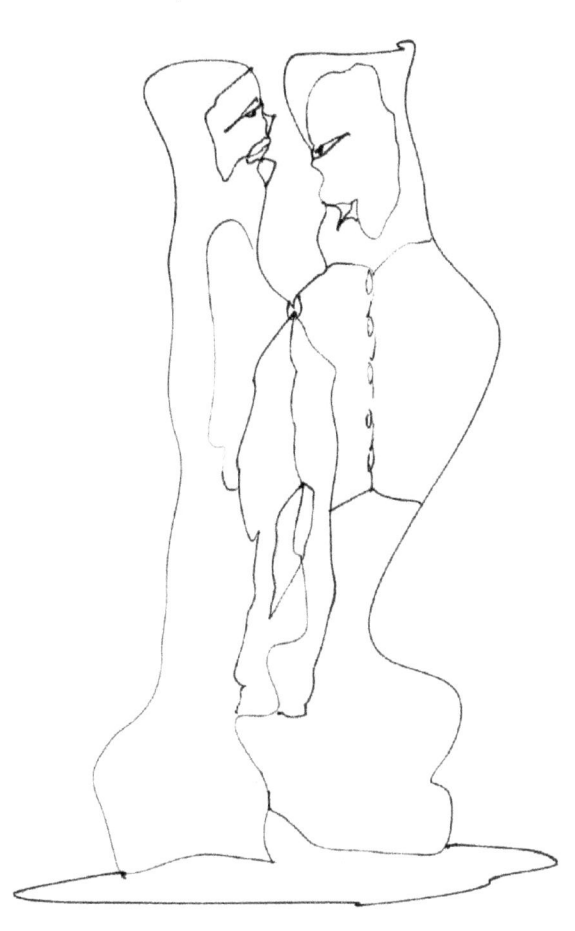

I have no roots.

My mood is of the air.

I cleave to nothing.

Those things I have are of me until they are no longer, until I am no longer.

Here on this wobbly mountain I have discovered a rhythm among the infinite changes occurring outside of me.

And now I flow more freely.

ABOUT THE AUTHOR

Peter Wells is a playwright, storyteller, and composer. Born in London, England, he spent his early years under the bombings of the German Blitz during WWII. He left England at the age of 20 and embarked on a journey in search of personal freedom and artistic fulfillment.

After traveling around the world, he settled in the rural hills of Northern California. Peter now lives in the coastal village of Mendocino, where he is a successful business owner, as well as a father of seven (grandfather of 8), and where he continues to pursue his passion for creating a harmonious way of life.

"We can more easily work together for shared benefits than against each other for shared suffering."

www.ingramcontent.com/pod-product-compliance
Lightning Source LLC
Chambersburg PA
CBHW061222070526
44584CB00029B/3941